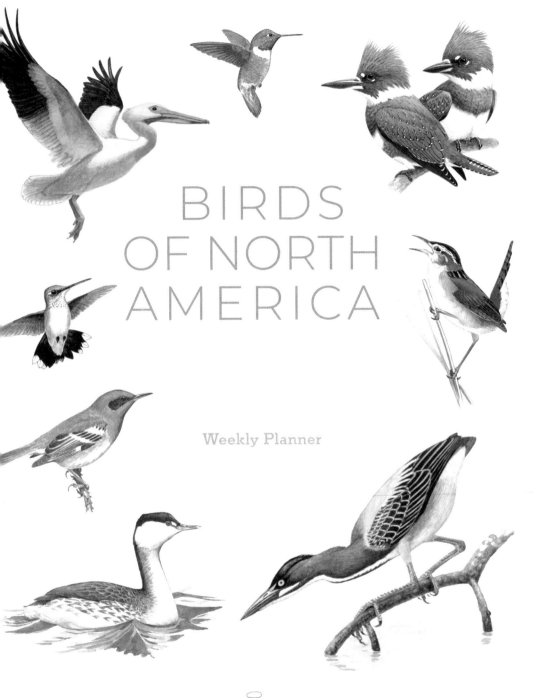

BIRDS
OF NORTH
AMERICA

Weekly Planner

ROCK
POINT

Before Taking Flight

Welcome nature enthusiasts, bird lovers, and scientists! If you have picked up this planner, you are destined for fascinating moments outdoors where it is sometimes a little noisy, surrounded by nature's best frequent fliers: birds.

North America in this book refers to the United States and Canada, so the birds featured reside in areas all over the country migrating, breeding, and wintering in forests, beaches, and backyards. With their beautiful and melodic songs creating the background of this highly populated land, we can thank those dedicated people who recorded bird sounds and maintained collections of their recordings for the information presented in this planner.

This book works as a multifunctional planner and an informative bird book, so bring it along on your birding adventures. Wherever you end up outdoors, learn to recognize the sounds as you discover the fascinating world of birds, both common and rare, and all their favorite foods, common quirks, and personalities.

In the back of this planner, we've left some space for you to document all the birds you see during your year of birding. But first, let's go over some things you may need to get started.

What You'll Need

Place(s): A natural area with enough biodiversity to support multiple species of birds. Choose someplace you can get to easily and visit regularly. Having more than one place for birding is the goal, but there's no shame in backyard birding, as many of us started out that way.

Equipment: Binoculars, spotting scopes, cameras, and recording devices. There are also apps that you can download, such as the Merlin Bird ID, eBird, and Audubon, to help you identify and keep track of the species you've observed. Having equipment is not necessary to be a birder, but if all else fails, a pair of binoculars goes a long way.

Time: The best way to make a new hobby stick is to have a routine. Once you've chosen your place(s), try to visit at least a few times each month. This will allow you to observe how the assemblage and activity of the birds in that area change throughout the seasons. Mornings are when most species are the most active, but if you want to spot owls, nightjars, and any of the more secretive marsh birds, you might try visiting at a different time.

By heeding the advice in this planner, you'll be a full-fledged birder whose passion can be found across the country. But a word of advice before you get your feet on the ground: Practice stillness, respect the birds and their habitats, and watch out for any droppings.

Northern Cardinal
Cardinalis cardinalis

Bird song: *purty purty purly*

The Northern Cardinal is a familiar, red-crested songbird found in the eastern half of the United States and in the extreme southwest.

The males are hard to miss thanks to their brilliant red plumage and black masks. The females are also incredibly colorful, with a brownish body and red accents. Both have crests on their heads that they raise when agitated and lower when resting.

Cardinals establish breeding territories in an array of habitats with shrubs and small trees. They are considered forest birds mainly because they frequent forests and forest edges, as well as woodlands, marshes, and stream edges. You can also find their signature red in hedgerows around agricultural fields, parks, and suburban gardens.

Females sing often while sitting on the nest. They do so to give information to the male about when they're hungry and need food brought to the nest. In this conversation, a mated pair shares song phrases, with the female singing longer and slightly more complex songs than the male.

A year-round resident, Northern Cardinals have developed a close association with people, breeding near their structures and taking food from their feeders. These pretty birds also have small populations in California and Hawaii due to human transportation. Catch them foraging on the ground and in shrubs and trees, consuming fruits, seeds, buds, and insects.

NOTES	SUNDAY	MONDAY	TUESDAY

WEDNESDAY	THURSDAY	FRIDAY	SATURDAY

Northern Cardinal Facts

Fun fact: If you live in one of their native regions, cardinals are one of the easiest birds to spot because they do not migrate. You can always rely on them being around if you share a hometown.

Close relative: Pyrrhuloxia *(Cardinalis sinuatus)*

Food: The shape of a cardinal's bill is specially formed for cutting and crushing shells to extract seeds. They also eat insects and fruit, and they'll visit just about any seed feeder.

Nesting: Cardinals generally make their homes 15 feet (4.5 m) or less from the ground in cup nests between two branches. The male gathers the materials while the female does most of the building.

Pyrrhuloxia

Bird song: Both male and female cardinals sing. Songs are typically pure-toned, whistled sounds: *what cheer, cheer, cheer; cheer, cheer, what what what what* or *purty purty purty*. Males sing during courtship and to defend their territories; females sing to communicate with mates and possibly to aggressively warn other females. The most frequently given calls of cardinals, which possess fifteen or more call types, are chips, used in many situations.

MONDAY

TUESDAY

WEDNESDAY

THURSDAY

FRIDAY

SATURDAY

SUNDAY

MONDAY

TUESDAY

WEDNESDAY

THURSDAY

FRIDAY

SATURDAY

SUNDAY

Pacific Loon

North America's most abundant loon, the species nests on freshwater
ponds throughout much of the arctic and subarctic tundra and in
forested regions of Alaska and northern Canada.

MONDAY

TUESDAY

WEDNESDAY

THURSDAY

FRIDAY

SATURDAY

SUNDAY

Barred Owl

Vocalizations of this owl are intriguing and
often rendered as "Who cooks for you?
Who cooks for you all?"

MONDAY

TUESDAY

WEDNESDAY

THURSDAY

FRIDAY

SATURDAY

SUNDAY

Pied-billed Grebe

The most extensive distribution in the Americas of any grebe, they breed from northern Canada through southern South America.

White-throated Sparrow

Zonotrichia albicollis

Bird song: *Oh, sweet Canada!*

The White-throated Sparrow is a songbird familiar to many, especially for its songs of pure, whistled tones and contrasting colors on the head and face plumage.

They winter principally in eastern and central North America and are migrants to western California. Breeding in much of Canada and the northeastern United States, they occupy coniferous and mixed deciduous-coniferous forests and woodlands, usually in dense, brushy vegetation, such as areas around bogs, ponds, and rocky outcrops. They winter in dense brush, sometimes in parks and urban areas. As regular seed-feeder visitors, they eat insects, seeds, and fruits.

The contrasting colors on their heads and faces are a fantastic sight, so keep a pair of binoculars handy. White-throated Sparrows have a broad range of browns, blacks, and grays on the body, with a white throat, black and white stripes on top of the head, and yellow patches above the eyes. Catch them hopping on both feet on the ground, where they scratch back leaf litter and then jump forward to pounce on their catch.

Coming from song neighborhoods, young male White-throated Sparrows learn their call by listening to the other males near them. Sometimes they'll add something new, either by accident or simply because they want to, and a new trend will begin.

NOTES	SUNDAY	MONDAY	TUESDAY

WEDNESDAY	THURSDAY	FRIDAY	SATURDAY

White-throated Sparrow Facts

Fun fact: The female builds the nest mostly in the mornings, finding a depression in the ground and building it up with pieces of moss. The nest is concealed from above by leaves and visible on only one side.

Food: These birds eat seeds and insects, so they will readily visit your backyards and seed feeders, especially in winter.

Bird song: The distinct *Oh, sweet Canada!* call of the male White-throated Sparrow might well be one of the first you start to recognize. To many people, it's the "call of winter," but it's also a great example of how some birds learn their calls from "song neighborhoods."

Male songs in this species function in territorial defense and mate attraction. Specifically, for mate attraction, the young males waver in their call, as if they're unsure whether they're doing it right. When they discover that their call no longer attracts females because a new variation has emerged, they either join the trend or create yet another new variation.

One documented song variation of male White-throated Sparrows originated in Prince George, British Columbia, and became such a forceful trend that it spread 1,800 miles (2,897 km) east in less than twenty years!

MONDAY

TUESDAY

WEDNESDAY

THURSDAY

FRIDAY

SATURDAY

SUNDAY

MONDAY

TUESDAY

WEDNESDAY

THURSDAY

FRIDAY

SATURDAY

SUNDAY

Merlin

A small, dashing falcon that breeds across North
America's northern forests and prairies, they lay
eggs in the abandoned nests of crows and hawks.

MONDAY

TUESDAY

WEDNESDAY

THURSDAY

FRIDAY

SATURDAY

SUNDAY

Wild Turkey

Strong short-distance fliers,
they roost in trees at night but
spend most daylight hours
on the ground.

MONDAY

TUESDAY

WEDNESDAY

THURSDAY

FRIDAY

SATURDAY

SUNDAY

California Quail

During the breeding season, members of the covey, or flock, branch out in pairs to nest and raise their young.

Whooping Crane
Grus americana

Bird song: *Glaaap!*

The Whooping Crane is now a national symbol of successful efforts to recover an endangered species. Returning from the brink of extinction, the species has increased from only fifteen or sixteen individuals in 1941 to several hundred today. It remains one of the rarest birds in North America.

The tallest bird in North America, some whoopers reach nearly 5 feet (1.5 m) with a 7-foot (2.1 m) wingspan. Seek out their smooth and stately gait from a good distance away. Very few of these cranes actually migrate, choosing to winter on the Texas coast of the Gulf of Mexico. A small population has also been established in central Florida.

Though some birds innately know the direction and distance to travel during a migration, others—like ducks, geese, and cranes—do not. They must learn their migratory route from older birds, and it can take several trips to do so. Because there were so few for so long and Whooping Cranes learn from family members, their historic migration routes have been forgotten.

These wetland birds are a monogamous bird, so after an elaborate courtship dance of leaping, kicking, head-pumping, and wing-sweeping, they create a small nesting territory, preferably on a small island in the marsh, where they pile up vegetation and then stomp it into a cozy nest.

NOTES	SUNDAY	MONDAY	TUESDAY

WEDNESDAY	THURSDAY	FRIDAY	SATURDAY

Whooping Crane Facts

Fun fact: Because there were so few for so long, Whooping Cranes forgot their historic migration routes. Instead, they had to relearn them by being released with huge flocks of Sandhill Cranes, with some even guided by humans in planes. The three reintroduced populations we have today exist because of these programs.

Food: Cranes feed primarily on land or in shallow marshes. Rather than hunting, they move at a stately pace, browsing and probing for food. Using their bills to probe the surface, they eat berries, seeds, insects, snails, reptiles, amphibians, nestling birds, and small mammals. They are also particularly fond of snails, clams, crayfish, and other crustaceans.

Nesting: The only self-sustaining wild population nests in Wood Buffalo National Park in the Northwest Territories of Canada. The male and female build the nest together by piling up and trampling vegetation such as bulrushes, sedges, and cattails. The nest can be 2 to 5 feet (0.6 to 1.5 m) across and has a flat surface or shallow depression for the eggs.

Bird song: Whooping Cranes produce ten or more call types, but the common name of the species probably derives from its guard call or unison call. The guard call is a loud call associated with aggression or fear, given as an individual approaches or threatens other cranes. Males and females use the unison call in a coordinated duet; it functions in pairing and pair-bond maintenance.

MONDAY

....

TUESDAY

....

WEDNESDAY

....

THURSDAY

....

FRIDAY

....

SATURDAY

....

SUNDAY

....

MONDAY

TUESDAY

WEDNESDAY

THURSDAY

FRIDAY

SATURDAY

SUNDAY

Say's Phoebe

A bird of open areas found across much of
western North American, they frequently nest
in abandoned buildings on prairie farms and
western ranches.

MONDAY

TUESDAY

WEDNESDAY

THURSDAY

White-eyed Vireo

A migratory songbird, they breed over
most of the eastern half of the United States,
where it is common in dense scrub, wood margins,
and overgrown pastures.

MONDAY

TUESDAY

WEDNESDAY

THURSDAY

FRIDAY

SATURDAY

SUNDAY

Black-billed Magpie

These magpies consume mostly insects, seeds, and carrion, but also small mammals, grain, and wild fruit; a major portion of their winter diet consists of vegetable matter.

MONDAY

TUESDAY

WEDNESDAY

THURSDAY

FRIDAY

SATURDAY

SUNDAY

Horned Lark

Hear them singing in flight, during courtship,
or from a perch, or on the ground,
when it may function as
territorial defense.

Black-capped Chickadee

Poecile atricapillus

Bird song: *fee-bee*

A common park bird across much of the northern United States and Canada, the Black-capped Chickadee is familiar to many, especially because it is a frequent bird-feeder visitor. The biggest gossip of the woodlands, they are quick to call out to their comrades to share new food sources. Many songbirds associate with chickadees due to their intelligence and ability to communicate different environmental conditions, including titmice, woodpeckers, nuthatches, creepers, kinglets, vireos, and warblers.

However, when it comes to their secret caches, their beaks are sealed. If a chickadee thinks it is being watched by a competitor, it'll pretend to make a new cache but hold on to the food until it's no longer being watched.

These chickadees have more personality than would seem capable for their roughly 5-inch (13 cm) long bodies. They are adorable birds, with a distinctive black cap that continues down their face to cover their throat, and have gray wings, tails, and backs, with white cheek patches and rusty flanks.

The species prefers deciduous and mixed deciduous-coniferous woodlands for a nesting cavity in a standing dead tree or branch selected by the female. She'll then use moss, grasses, or other materials to make a cup-shaped nest and line it with soft materials, like fur. Chickadees also readily take to human-made nest boxes under the right conditions.

NOTES	SUNDAY	MONDAY	TUESDAY

WEDNESDAY	THURSDAY	FRIDAY	SATURDAY

Black-capped Chickadee

Fun fact: Despite their size, Black-capped Chickadees and their cousins are very intelligent. They have more than ten complex calls that form their own language and can remember thousands of hidden food caches. Chickadees constantly adapt to new social and environmental factors by replacing neurons in their brains to keep their minds sharp.

Food: Taking most of its food from tree leaves and twigs, they sometimes hang at odd angles or upside down to grab prey. Their diet consists of insects, spiders, seeds, and small fruits.

Nesting: Nest boxes attract a breeding pair when it is placed well before breeding season. Place it at least 60 feet (18 m) into a wooded area. It must have a guard to keep predators from raiding eggs and young. Chickadees are also attracted to sawdust or wood shavings.

Bird song: The *chick-a-dee-dee-dee* call, given by both sexes, has many functions, including providing information about identity and describing factors in their environment, from food availability and type to predator location and level of threat.

The loud *fee-bee* call, usually two or three whistled notes, uttered chiefly by males, plays a role in leading flocks and advertising territories. Another call, the *gargle,* is used primarily by males in aggressive as well as some sexual situations.

MONDAY

TUESDAY

WEDNESDAY

THURSDAY

FRIDAY

SATURDAY

SUNDAY

MONDAY

TUESDAY

WEDNESDAY

THURSDAY

FRIDAY

SATURDAY

SUNDAY

Yellow-breasted Chat

At about 7½ inches (19 cm) long,
the chat is the largest of North America's
more than forty-five warbler species.

MONDAY

TUESDAY

WEDNESDAY

THURSDAY

Palm Warbler

Most of its warbler relatives are denizens of forest
canopies, but this interesting bird prefers
open areas with scattered trees, dense
shrubby habitats, and bogs.

MONDAY

TUESDAY

WEDNESDAY

THURSDAY

Common Yellowthroat

Wintering in the southern United States, the
Caribbean, and Latin America, they breed
in and around marshes; wet, overgrown fields;
drainage ditches; and orchards.

Chimney Swift
Chaetura pelagica

Bird song: *chip*

Chimney Swifts are small, all-dark swifts with a reputation for flying fast and being highly maneuverable in the air. They breed mainly across the eastern half of North America, wintering in South America.

Often described as "flying cigars," Chimney Swifts spend the vast majority of their lives on the wing, nimbly maneuvering overhead. These strange birds circle the skies with their high, chattering calls, foraging in midair for insects from the moment they wake until roosting time. Chimney Swifts are often most noticeable during migration, when they circle in large flocks, sometimes numbering in the thousands.

Although they are common in more urban settings, their numbers have declined by roughly 67 percent over the last sixty years, most likely due to the declining availability of brick chimneys to rest on. If a Chimney Swift does take up residence in your brick chimney, it's a good idea to keep the damper closed during the summer and schedule cleanings either before or after the breeding season. To help their population, you can build a swift nesting tower with plans from the North American Chimney Swift Nest Site Research Project.

While they will roost together, they aren't colony nesters. Mated pairs strike out on their own when they're ready to build a nest, but they still sometimes welcome nonbreeders into their new home. Sometimes, these unmated visitors even help raise the young.

NOTES	SUNDAY	MONDAY	TUESDAY

WEDNESDAY	THURSDAY	FRIDAY	SATURDAY

Chimney Swift Facts

Fun fact: Because they're unable to perch, they use their long, specialized claws and spiny tail feathers to cling to vertical walls inside hollow trees, caves, and (as you might have guessed) chimneys when they need a rest. During the nonbreeding season, large numbers of Chimney Swifts often roost together in a single cavity to conserve heat.

Swifts even bathe in flight. Without stopping, they glide down to the water and crash against the surface before flying up and shaking the water off their bodies.

Food: Their days are spent in wide-ranging, fast flights in pursuit of their favorite food: flying insects.

Nesting: These swifts have a gland under their tongues that produces sticky saliva, which they use as glue to attach their nests to a cavity wall. Both the male and the female gather materials for the nest independently. They break off small twigs with their tiny feet and carry them back to the nesting site of hollow trees, chimneys, and the walls of abandoned buildings.

Bird song: Little is known about Chimney Swift's vocalizations. They produce a series of high-pitched chip calls, which are apparently used in a variety of contexts. In flight, the chips are sometimes so close together that they become a buzzy insect-like twitter. Young swifts make rasping *raah, raah, raah* calls.

MONDAY

TUESDAY

WEDNESDAY

THURSDAY

FRIDAY

SATURDAY

SUNDAY

MONDAY

TUESDAY

WEDNESDAY

THURSDAY

FRIDAY

SATURDAY

SUNDAY

Lincoln's Sparrow

Relatively little is known about this sparrow's behavior because of its preference for dense shrub cover, often breeding at higher elevations over vast stretches of Alaska and Canada.

MONDAY

TUESDAY

WEDNESDAY

THURSDAY

FRIDAY

SATURDAY

SUNDAY

Lapland Longspur

A handsome, strong-flying sparrow-like bird that
breeds in tundra habitats of Alaska and northern
Canada; the name "longspur" refers to the
long claw on the hind toe.

MONDAY

TUESDAY

WEDNESDAY

THURSDAY

FRIDAY

SATURDAY

SUNDAY

Bobolink

A long-distance migrant that inhabits grassland
environments, primarily across broad swaths of the
northern United States and southern Canada, wintering
in the pampas grasslands of South America.

Indigo Bunting
Passerina cyanea

Bird song: *ti ti whee whee zerre zerre*

Male

Common and brightly colored, the Indigo Bunting is a familiar small songbird across the eastern and central United States and southeastern Canada. By early summer, one can often look to the highest perch in a particular area and find a male Indigo Bunting there, broadcasting his song over the landscape.

A drive down a gravel road next to a woodland edge may reveal a splash of brown and the bluest blue imaginable. Males are an incredibly rich, deep blue, while juvenile males and females are brownish. The most common sighting is after foraging, when they take off from the ground for the safety of trees.

Their breeding territories are often established in woodland clearings and in brushy habitats along the margins of woods, roads, and agricultural lands. They forage on the ground, in bushes, and in trees. When the nesting season is over and it is time to migrate, Indigo Buntings winter mainly in Mexico, Central America, the Caribbean, and northern South America.

The enthusiastically singing male Indigo Buntings, like many other songbirds such as White-crowned Sparrows, learn their songs in song neighborhoods. This means buntings a few hundred yards apart can sing different songs, while those in the same song neighborhood share nearly identical songs. A local song may persist for up to twenty years, changing gradually as new singers add different variations.

NOTES	SUNDAY	MONDAY	TUESDAY

WEDNESDAY	THURSDAY	FRIDAY	SATURDAY

Indigo Bunting Facts

Fun fact: During their journey to winter in Latin America, Indigo Buntings migrate at night, looking at the night sky and using memorized star patterns to guide them on their way. The idea that a creature that is smaller than a cell phone uses the stars to navigate a flight to a different continent seems unbelievable, but we often underestimate the intelligence and abilities of those around us.

Plumage: Like all other blue birds, they lack blue pigment. Their jewellike color is instead refracted off of structures in the feathers that reflect blue light, much like how the sky looks blue when it actually isn't.

Food: Indigo Buntings prefer small seeds and insects, such as buds, berries, and spiders, and generally look for them close to the ground. You may be able to attract them to feeders with thistle (such as the seed nyjer) or by setting out live mealworms.

Bird song: The song of a male Indigo Bunting advertises its territory to other males and to potential mates. This song consists of a sequence of high warbling notes, often in pairs rendered as *ti ti whee whee zerre zerre*. Brief calls of these birds include *chip*, given in many situations; *tink*, an alarm call; and *aaaa*, a threat signal.

Female

MONDAY

TUESDAY

WEDNESDAY

THURSDAY

FRIDAY

SATURDAY

SUNDAY

MONDAY

TUESDAY

WEDNESDAY

THURSDAY

FRIDAY

SATURDAY

SUNDAY

Rock Pigeon

Now feral and breeding throughout the United
States and southern Canada; around humans they
consume bread, currants, popcorn, peanuts,
French fries, and cake.

MONDAY

TUESDAY

WEDNESDAY

THURSDAY

Willow Ptarmigan

The largest and most numerous of North America's
three ptarmigan species, and characteristic of the
arctic and subarctic tundras.

MONDAY

TUESDAY

WEDNESDAY

THURSDAY

FRIDAY

SATURDAY

SUNDAY

American Kestrel

Formerly known as the Sparrow Hawk, they
eat primarily insects and small rodents
captured on the ground.

MONDAY

TUESDAY

WEDNESDAY

THURSDAY

FRIDAY

SATURDAY

SUNDAY

Ring-necked Pheasant

A popular game bird throughout agricultural lands from southern Canada to California on the West Coast and the New England states on the East.

Wood Thrush

Hylocichla mustelina

Bird song: *cheer-uu-lee*

A larger, stocky thrush of deciduous and mixed deciduous-coniferous forests, the Wood Thrush is often rendered conspicuous by its beautiful, ethereal vocalizations. Yet its strange, harmonizing call makes it famous.

With their reddish-brown backs and white, speckled bellies, the plumage of the Wood Thrush is unassuming. This lack of flashiness in the plumage is summed up well in their scientific name, *Hylocichla mustelina*, meaning "weasel-colored woodland thrush." Spot one of these secretive birds standing upright, with a relaxed, plump white belly showing dark spots. A rusty red cape extends from the head down the back to the end of the tail.

The species breeds throughout the eastern woodlands of the United States and adjacent parts of southeastern Canada, and it winters in Mexico and Central America, enjoying the tropical forests there. They enjoy berries and fruits from plants like elderberry, holly, and pokeweed. If you'd like to see or hear a thrush and are further west than central North America, you may have a chance to observe a Swainson's Thrush, a relative that is also an amazing songster.

Male songs, which have roles in territorial defense and mate attraction, are comprised of a series of three or four clear, fluty phrases separated by pauses and ending with a trill, sometimes sounding like *cheer-uu-lee . . . cheer-uu-lee-ah . . . ch-cheero-cheero-lee*. When disturbed, these thrushes give *bup-bup* alert calls; when disturbances become threats, they produce *pit-pit* alarm calls.

NOTES	SUNDAY	MONDAY	TUESDAY

WEDNESDAY	THURSDAY	FRIDAY	SATURDAY

Wood Thrush Facts

Fun fact: Despite its beautiful song, this bird is quite a reclusive creature, spending much of its time on the ground foraging leaf litter. Their cinnamon-brown upperparts grant them great camouflage, and they are unlikely to come to feeders.

Food: Calcium is an important mineral females require to lay a clutch of eggs. They need ten to fifteen times more calcium than normal, making calcium-rich food supplements, like snail shells, pivotal during their breeding season.

Nesting: Wood Thrushes are vulnerable to nest parasitism by Brown-headed Cowbirds, who will lay their eggs in other birds' nests and expect them to raise the young. In some Midwest forest edges, virtually every Wood Thrush nest contains at least one cowbird egg.

Brown-headed Cowbird

Bird song: The harmonizing call of this bird makes it famous. To create their strange, harmonizing call, it sings two notes simultaneously using its Y-shaped voice. While singing two notes at once is actually quite common among songbirds, few do so in a way that humans can hear. For example, Northern Cardinals make two sounds at once for their call, but you wouldn't be able to distinguish it. Wood Thrushes' standard vocalizations are a variety of *Ree-ert!* and *Rap, rap, reedle-deet!* sounds.

MONDAY

TUESDAY

WEDNESDAY

THURSDAY

FRIDAY

SATURDAY

SUNDAY

MONDAY

TUESDAY

WEDNESDAY

THURSDAY

FRIDAY

SATURDAY

SUNDAY

Chestnut-sided Warbler

One of the most abundant warblers, they nest
in areas of regrowing woods, breeding in
the northeastern United States and central and
southeastern Canada.

MONDAY

TUESDAY

WEDNESDAY

THURSDAY

FRIDAY

SATURDAY

SUNDAY

Phainopepla

In brushy desert breeding areas, mated pairs nest
alone, but at woodland breeding sites, they often nest in
loose colonies made of three to fifteen pairs.

MONDAY

TUESDAY

WEDNESDAY

THURSDAY

FRIDAY

SATURDAY

SUNDAY

American Robin

Known for its persistent singing in spring,
its lawn-stalking of earthworms, its "robin
red-breast" chest, and its blue eggs.

Red-winged Blackbird

Agelaius phoeniceus

Bird song: *conk-a-ree*

Male

The Red-winged Blackbird, a marsh breeder, is one of North America's most abundant songbirds. They are often seen on tall grasses in muddy roadsides and ditches; during the breeding season, find them in parts of Alaska, across much of Canada, and throughout the lower United States. Males can be seen perched atop cattails and other marshy plants in wetland areas. Some populations are migratory, but others are year-round residents.

Males, larger than females, are jet black with red and yellow shoulder patches, called epaulets. They can either hide or show off their epaulets depending on how confident they are of their dominance among other males in the landscape.

When the nesting season begins, males spread out across a marshy area with tall vegetation and stake their claim of a territory. They are known for their polygamous breeding system in which ten females may nest on the territory of a single male. The females will lay one or two clutches of two to four eggs through the season, which may or may not be sired by the male in whose territory she resides.

Into the fall and winter, Red-winged Blackbirds will form enormous multispecies flocks with other blackbirds, including grackles, cowbirds, and starlings. They can be seen moving in huge groups, thousands of birds strong, through agricultural fields in search of waste grain and seeds. Sometimes, they can cause significant harm to these areas.

NOTES	SUNDAY	MONDAY	TUESDAY

WEDNESDAY	THURSDAY	FRIDAY	SATURDAY

Red-winged Blackbird Facts

Fun fact: The level of sexual dimorphism (difference in appearance between males and females) is so high that often the brown, dark-streaked females are confused for some sort of large sparrow.

Food: They feed on the ground, on floating objects, and on vegetation, taking insects, seeds, and waste grain. You can probably attract them to feeders or by spreading seed on the ground, but rest assured, you will need a lot of birdseed for these large flocks.

Nesting: The females weave a nest of stems and coarse vegetation to make a platform. They add structure by piling wet leaves and mud to make a small bowl and then line the bowl nest with fine materials like grass.

Bird song: Male Red-winged Blackbirds each sing several versions of their familiar *conk-a-ree* or *o-ka-lee* song, each ending with a buzzy trill. These songs have roles in territory maintenance, as well as mate attraction and signaling.

Female

Females have two common songs, one a chittering sound, directed at their mates, and one a harsher buzzy sound, aggressively uttered at other females.

Both males and females have an array of calls, with *check* being the most common.

MONDAY

TUESDAY

WEDNESDAY

THURSDAY

FRIDAY

SATURDAY

SUNDAY

MONDAY

TUESDAY

WEDNESDAY

THURSDAY

FRIDAY

SATURDAY

SUNDAY

Hawaii Amakihi

These famous honeycreepers are found on Maui,
Molokai, and the Big Island of Hawaii, generally
in middle- and higher-elevation forests.

MONDAY

TUESDAY

WEDNESDAY

THURSDAY

FRIDAY

SATURDAY

SUNDAY

Pine Siskin

An inhabitant of coniferous or
mixed deciduous-coniferous forests,
they breed as far north as central Alaska
and northern Canada.

MONDAY

TUESDAY

WEDNESDAY

THURSDAY

FRIDAY

SATURDAY

SUNDAY

'Apapane

Both sexes vocalize throughout the year
using a diverse array of songs and calls, some
of which have roles in defending resources and in
male-female communication.

Wood Duck

Aix sponsa

Bird song: *ji-hib*

Male

One of the globe's most gorgeous ducks, the Wood Duck is a common denizen of wooded swamps, freshwater marshes, and slow-moving rivers. The species occurs in many of the contiguous forty-eight states and in southern Canada.

The males, with their distinctive facial pattern and iridescent green and purple head, take high honors as beautiful waterbirds. Females only have slightly crested heads with a white teardrop around the eye. But like many other ducks, the female does the main vocalizations of the species.

The bodies of Wood Ducks are fairly slim, most likely because they nest not in coastal or marsh vegetation but in natural cavities with small openings, such as tree holes made by large woodpeckers. If you wander around the swamps and sloughs, you may accidentally flush a pair, which will then take off together down the slough while the female makes a *Brr-eet! Brr-eet!* call.

In the water, they feed in small dives, turning upside down and grabbing food in a behavior known as "dabbling." When they can't find enough aquatic food, they will forage on land for acorns, nuts, and grains.

Wood Ducks readily take to human-provided nest boxes. While they have many nesting preferences, they also engage in a behavior known as "egg dumping" (or intraspecific brood parasitism), wherein they will lay eggs in another Wood Duck pair's nest cavity and have them raise their offspring as their own.

NOTES	SUNDAY	MONDAY	TUESDAY

WEDNESDAY	THURSDAY	FRIDAY	SATURDAY

Wood Duck Facts

Fun fact: Because ducklings can't fly yet, to get to the water below and begin their lives, they must make an amazing leap. After dropping dozens of feet to the ground, they simply bounce, dust themselves off, and waddle on their way.

Food: They eat seeds, fruits, aquatic and terrestrial beetles, flies, snails, and other small animals.

Nesting: Rather than ground-nesting like many of their cousins, mated pairs of Wood Ducks will search together high in trees for cavities. They can't excavate their own, so they look for one created by a limb that has broken off a trunk. The male then stands guard outside while the female prepares the cavity to her liking.

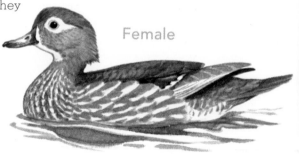

Female

Bird song: The basic call of male Wood Ducks, used to keep individuals in contact, is a drawn-out whistled *ji-hib* or a low, squeaky *jeeb*. The male burp call, which consists of short *pfits* often linked together in a series, draws attention during courtship, but it is also used as a warning signal.

The female *hauk* call—a loud *oo-eek*—is perhaps the most familiar vocalization of Wood Ducks, often given when females take flight after being disturbed.

MONDAY

TUESDAY

WEDNESDAY

THURSDAY

FRIDAY

SATURDAY

SUNDAY

MONDAY

TUESDAY

WEDNESDAY

THURSDAY

FRIDAY

SATURDAY

SUNDAY

'Elepaio

A forest bird that inhabits a variety of dry and
seasonally wet forests. Hawaiians note that they are
often the first birds to sing in the morning.

MONDAY

TUESDAY

WEDNESDAY

THURSDAY

FRIDAY

SATURDAY

SUNDAY

Clark's Nutcracker

Native to the mountains of the western
United States and Canada, they use their
sharp bill to open pinecones and extract their seeds.

MONDAY

TUESDAY

WEDNESDAY

THURSDAY

FRIDAY

SATURDAY

SUNDAY

Eastern Wood-Pewee

A small, generally inconspicuous flycatcher best
known for its tireless hawking flights after
insects and its plaintive song.

MONDAY

TUESDAY

WEDNESDAY

THURSDAY

FRIDAY

SATURDAY

SUNDAY

Ruddy Duck

A small, stocky, stiff-tailed duck
that breeds primarily in the
prairie pothole region of
North America.

Northern Flicker

Colaptes auratus

Bird song: *wik-wik-wik*

A common woodpecker that forages primarily on the ground, the Northern Flicker lives in most wooded regions of North America. A species of open woodlands, savannas, and forest edges, these woodpeckers are well adapted for human habitats, commonly breeding in urban as well as suburban and rural environments.

Like most woodpeckers, Northern Flickers drum on objects as a form of communication and territory defense. In such cases, the objective is to make as loud a noise as possible, hence why woodpeckers sometimes drum on metal objects.

Northern Flickers are the strange outliers of the woodpecker family. Instead of the flashy black, white, and red plumage of most of their brethren, the flicker's beauty is subtler. Keep your eyes peeled for the distinctive white patch on their rump. If you happen to catch one in flight, you'll immediately notice the incredible color in their wings.

There are two different forms of Northern Flickers: the yellow-shafted in eastern, central, and northern North America, and the red-shafted in Mexico, Central America, and the West. The main difference in plumage between these forms is the color of the shafts on the underside of the flight feathers and tail. Males of the yellow-shafted form will have a black streak on the cheek, called a malar stripe, while red-shafted males will have a red streak. Females look very similar, but they lack the malar stripe.

NOTES | SUNDAY | MONDAY | TUESDAY

WEDNESDAY	THURSDAY	FRIDAY	SATURDAY

Northern Flicker Facts

Fun facts: Another thing that makes Northern Flickers different from their woodpecker cousins is that they forage the ground for their favorite food source: ants. Not many woodpeckers migrate either, but Northern Flickers do. While they are present year-round across most of North America, they migrate during the nonbreeding season toward the southern parts.

Food: They eat mainly ants but also beetle larvae and a variety of berries and seeds. Their tongues can dart out 2 inches (5 cm) beyond the end of the bill to snare prey.

Nesting: The species usually excavates nest cavities in dead or diseased tree trunks. Sometimes, they will return to a cavity they (or another woodpecker) have already excavated. But unlike most woodpeckers, some flickers forgo trees altogether, choosing instead to nest underground in the previously used burrows of Belted Kingfishers. Their nests can be 6 to 15 feet (1.8 to 4.5 m) off the ground, but on some rare occasions, they can be over 100 feet (30 m) high.

Bird song: The most familiar Northern Flicker vocalization, *wik-wik-wik* or *kick, kick, kick,* is commonly heard in the springtime during pair formation and territory establishment. They give a wicka call, variably described as *wik-a, wik-a, wik-a* or *ta-week, ta-week, ta-week,* in a variety of situations. Flickers also communicate through drumming, produced when they rapidly hit wood with their bills.

MONDAY

TUESDAY

WEDNESDAY

THURSDAY

FRIDAY

SATURDAY

SUNDAY

MONDAY

TUESDAY

WEDNESDAY

THURSDAY

FRIDAY

SATURDAY

SUNDAY

American Dipper

A small, stocky songbird that lives
along streams and feeds on aquatic
insects, small fish, and fish eggs, foraging
almost entirely in streams.

MONDAY

TUESDAY

WEDNESDAY

THURSDAY

FRIDAY

SATURDAY

SUNDAY

Belted Kingfisher

Across the continent, they inhabit
diverse aquatic habitats where they
typically perch over clear, open water before
plunge-diving for prey, chiefly fish.

MONDAY

TUESDAY

WEDNESDAY

THURSDAY

FRIDAY

SATURDAY

SUNDAY

Tufted Puffin

A truly open-ocean species that spends much of its
life in the Pacific Ocean at great distances from land. It
is often quiet, only uttering some low growling sounds at
breeding colonies.

Great Horned Owl
Bubo virginianus

Bird song: *who-hoo-ho-oo*

The Great Horned Owl, a year-round resident throughout the United States and most of Canada, is a large, powerful bird that survives in almost any climate; it seems equally at home in desert, grassland, suburban, and forest habitats.

Its enormous yellow eyes allow for superb night vision, supporting its vocation as a fearsome nocturnal predator. Females are noticeably larger, while males have a deeper voice. In general, these are very large owls with large ear tufts (special hearing feathers) and a distinct white throat patch that can be seen while they are vocalizing or panting to get rid of excess heat.

The Great Horned Owls' breeding season consists of several months of simply roosting together before laying eggs. Great Horned Owls will claim an already-made raptor nest and make their recognizable, soft *who-hoo-ho-oo* to let the other owls know it is now theirs.

These iconic, mostly solitary birds generally mate for life, so it takes them more time to find a suitable partner. They must depend on each other throughout the winter because the incubation of a single brood of one to four eggs takes more than a month. They persevere and dedicate a lot of work and time to such a small number of offspring because with the amount of time it takes for them to raise their young, there may not be enough time to start over if the first brood fails.

NOTES	SUNDAY	MONDAY	TUESDAY

WEDNESDAY	THURSDAY	FRIDAY	SATURDAY

Great Horned Owl Facts

Fun fact: Without encouraging violence, it would be best to bet on these owls in a fight against large prey, for they are fierce predators. They can take on ospreys, Peregrine Falcons, Prairie Falcons, and other owls. Comically though, that doesn't stop American Crows from harassing them for hours. The Great Horned Owl is their most dangerous predator, but they choose not to back down or cower in fear.

Food: These owls take a variety of prey, from scorpions and small rodents to larger hares and rabbits, and even large birds such as ducks, herons, and even other owls. Catching small prey is all thanks to their large eyes with excellent night vision.

Nesting: Because most other birds will have abandoned their nests by fall, Great Horned Owls usually claim an already-made raptor nest as their own and hoot to let the other owls know it is now theirs. These birds will then spend the next several months caring for their young. The female will incubate the eggs, and the male will bring her food.

Bird song: Territorial hoots are advertisement calls that sound like distant foghorns: *who-hoo-ho-oo* or *who-ho-o-o, whoo-hoo-o-o, whoo.* When disturbed and during nest defense, the owls produce short, barking utterances. Piercing screaming calls indicate stress or danger and are especially pronounced during nest defense.

MONDAY

TUESDAY

WEDNESDAY

THURSDAY

FRIDAY

SATURDAY

SUNDAY

MONDAY

TUESDAY

WEDNESDAY

THURSDAY

FRIDAY

SATURDAY

SUNDAY

Ruddy Turnstone

One of the most northerly breeding species of
shorebirds, they nest in the northernmost tundra
regions in Alaska and across arctic Canada, and
winter along the Atlantic, Pacific, and Gulf coasts.

MONDAY

TUESDAY

WEDNESDAY

THURSDAY

FRIDAY

SATURDAY

SUNDAY

American Avocet

Generally, they feed by wading in open shallow
water, using their highly sensitive bills to catch
prey or to probe into the water to snatch anything that
touches their bills.

MONDAY

TUESDAY

WEDNESDAY

THURSDAY

FRIDAY

SATURDAY

SUNDAY

Black Oystercatcher

Large, blackish shorebirds found in rocky intertidal
areas along the West Coast of North America, they
depend completely on shorelines for food and breeding.

Northern Harrier

Circus cyaneus

Bird song: kek-kek-kek-kek

The Northern Harrier is a slim, medium-sized raptor with a white rump that frequents grasslands and both freshwater and saltwater marshes. Formerly called the Marsh Hawk, it is often seen flying low, using its feathered ears to search for food more similar to owls than to its fellow hawks.

This species is widespread, with breeding populations in fields and marshes across most of North America. Harriers in middle North American latitudes are year-round residents. When migratory populations in the far north are forced to head south, harriers tend to do so alone during the day, hunting on the journey until they find a place that does not have a harrier yet.

In winter, these birds roost together, and often with Short-eared Owls. They nest on the ground, usually in tall, dense clumps of vegetation. Harrier sexes are easy to tell apart: Males are gray above and whitish below, and females are brown above and light and heavily streaked below.

Males perform aerial acrobatics to impress the females during courtship. They'll fly high into the air, and then show off with a series of barrel rolls. The males typically bring the nesting materials to the females, who then arrange them in the nest. Mated pairs aren't necessarily monogamous; in fact, some males will mate with up to five females during one breeding season.

NOTES	SUNDAY	MONDAY	TUESDAY

WEDNESDAY	THURSDAY	FRIDAY	SATURDAY

Northern Harrier Facts

Fun fact: The males have a "gray ghost" look due to their cloudy plumage. Both juveniles and females are a deep, mottled brown with lighter undersides, but you can distinguish the females by their dark brown eyes. Juveniles, on the other hand, have pale, yellow eyes.

Food: They eat small mammals (primarily rodents), birds, reptiles, and frogs.

Nesting: Males can have between two and five mates at once. The nest is built on the ground with a dense clump of vegetation. Building the nest takes one to two weeks, and measures 16 to 18 inches (40 to 46 cm) wide by 1½ to 8 inches (4 to 20 cm) high.

Bird song: Northern Harriers emit a variety of calls, and they are especially vocal near their nests. In courtship displays, both sexes utter *kek, quik,* or *ek* sounds in rapid series. The distress call is a more urgent, high-pitched *kek* or *ke*, also uttered in rapid succession. The female gives this call if she's disturbed at the nest (by ground predators, raptors, or humans), and it often attracts her mate, who then joins in calling.

During the breeding season, females issue their food call, a piercing, descending scream, *eeyah eeyah*. She almost always gives this call, which may be repeated for minutes in the presence of the mate, apparently in an effort to induce him to turn over food or to stimulate him to hunt.

MONDAY

TUESDAY

WEDNESDAY

THURSDAY

FRIDAY

SATURDAY

SUNDAY

MONDAY

TUESDAY

WEDNESDAY

THURSDAY

Snow Goose

One of the most abundant species
of waterfowl in the world, as well as
one of the noisiest, they breed in dense colonies along the coast and on
islands in arctic and subarctic Canada.

MONDAY

TUESDAY

WEDNESDAY

THURSDAY

FRIDAY

SATURDAY

SUNDAY

Roseate Spoonbill

In the United States, these birds are largely limited to
Florida and the Gulf Coast, where they frequent shallow
aquatic habitats, both inland and along the coast.

MONDAY

TUESDAY

WEDNESDAY

THURSDAY

FRIDAY

SATURDAY

SUNDAY

Black-crowned Night Heron

Common in many parts of North America, they also
breed on every continent except Australia and Antarctica.

MONDAY

TUESDAY

WEDNESDAY

THURSDAY

Bald Eagle

Eagles feed on a variety of mammals, birds,
and reptiles, and they're notorious pirates,
often taking food from ospreys, other eagles,
and humans.

Cedar Waxwing

Bombycilla cedrorum

Bird song: *bzeee*

The Cedar Waxwing is a beautiful, common, crested bird. It breeds in the woodlands over the southern half of Canada and the northern half of the United States. Widespread across North America, some migrate to southern Canada in the summer and spend their winters all across the southern United States, into Mexico and Central America.

Named for the red, waxlike tips on the ends of their wings, these birds are incredibly beautiful. They are known for their flocking and often nomadic movements as they search for food. Their favorite food is predominately sugary, ripe fruits taken from trees and shrubs. Waxwings also feed on insects during summer, taking them from vegetation and also from the air, like flycatchers.

If you have a berry bush, such as a holly, in your yard, you may have already seen flocks of these birds bombing them for fruit. They become a truly unruly mob in search of it. These birds eat so much fruit that they will sometimes consume berries that have already begun to ferment, resulting in drunkenness.

Lacking true songs, this songbird possesses only brief calls. The two main categories are trill-like calls and high-pitched, hissy whistled notes. But not to downplay their singing abilities, waxwings can produce up to seven different trill-like calls, used in various contexts.

NOTES	SUNDAY	MONDAY	TUESDAY

WEDNESDAY	THURSDAY	FRIDAY	SATURDAY

Cedar Waxwing Facts

Fun fact: When feeding on fruits, they pluck them one by one and swallow the entire thing whole.

Close relative: Another member of the Bombycillidae family, or waxwing family, is the Bohemian Waxwing. They are intriguing songbirds as, like their brethren, they lack true songs. They breed in Alaska and northern Canada and winter in the northern United States and southern Canada.

Food: These birds often go to battle over fruits. Often, Northern Mockingbirds claim berry bushes as their own for the winter, but this doesn't stop Cedar Waxwings from trying to steal straight out from under them. The mockingbird will move from one side of the bush to the other trying to scare the flock of waxwings away. In a sort of dance battle, the waxwings simply move to the other side, defiant in claiming the fruit, until the mockingbird tires and lets them have what they seek.

Bohemian Waxwing

Nesting: Females decide where they want to make the nest and they do almost all of the building. Choosing a branch from anywhere between 3 to 50 feet (0.9 to 15 m) high, the female weaves twigs, grasses, blossoms, string, and similar materials into a bulky cup. She then lines the cup with fine roots, grasses, and pine needles.

MONDAY

TUESDAY

WEDNESDAY

THURSDAY

FRIDAY

SATURDAY

SUNDAY

MONDAY

TUESDAY

WEDNESDAY

THURSDAY

FRIDAY

SATURDAY

SUNDAY

Red Crossbill

A nomadic bird found around
conifer forests from southern Alaska and
western and southern Canada south to
Arizona and California.

MONDAY

TUESDAY

WEDNESDAY

THURSDAY

FRIDAY

SATURDAY

SUNDAY

Golden-crowned Sparrow

A large, handsome sparrow that
only breeds in shrubby tundra
habitats and deciduous thickets in
Alaska and western Canada.

MONDAY

TUESDAY

WEDNESDAY

THURSDAY

FRIDAY

SATURDAY

SUNDAY

Red-shouldered Hawk

This hawk hunts from a perch, waiting for its prey to reveal itself and then swoops down to snatch it from the ground or water.

American Crow
Corvus brachyrhynchos

Bird song: *Caw!*

One of North America's most familiar—and often unpopular—birds, the American Crow is a smart and very prominent avian presence over much of the continent. They are an adaptable genus, and their incredible level of intelligence makes for an easy life.

Mainly, they live in open environments, both natural and man-made. They forage alone, in pairs, in families, or in flocks, eating almost anything: insects, amphibians, reptiles, small birds and mammals, seeds, fruits, crops, carrion, and garbage.

American Crows are social creatures, happily spending time foraging for food and roosting together, not just with their family groups but also with any crow around. Spending most of their time with other crows, they are endlessly curious about the world around them, figuring out new ways to acquire food and learning from each other. After they learn something new, they are quick to teach their friends the new trick, too, whether it's about new food items or a new food location.

To nest, they tend to look for a coniferous tree and build the nest near the top, close to the trunk. Nesting becomes more of a family business for American Crows and many other Corvids, with young from previous clutches of a mated pair staying and helping prepare the nest. These older siblings help raise their younger siblings well into their fourth year before finally striking out to make a family of their own.

NOTES	SUNDAY	MONDAY	TUESDAY

WEDNESDAY	THURSDAY	FRIDAY	SATURDAY

American Crow Facts

Fun fact: Older siblings often stay well into their fourth year before finally striking out to make a family of their own.

Food: Though they don't tend to stay deep in the woodland interior, they are intelligent enough to recognize reliable food sources, from grains to insects to aquatic animals. They are also nest predators, eating the eggs and nestlings of many species.

Nesting: Both members of a breeding pair help build the nest. They typically hide it tucked near the trunk and towards the top of the tree. They prefer evergreens, but deciduous trees will suffice. Made of medium-sized twigs, they line the inner cup with pine needles, weeds, soft bark, or animal hair. A pair will often lay one to two broods of three to nine eggs each.

Bird song: American Crows vocalize when perched, on the ground, and in flight. Their most common call is *caw,* which is given in various ways and in different situations: Some caws are general alarm calls, some are used when mobbing predators, some are used to call other crows to assist in mobbing, and some are territorial advertisements. The species' other calls include rattles and calls that sound like *cawl, caa,* and *kr-aack.*

MONDAY

TUESDAY

WEDNESDAY

THURSDAY

FRIDAY

SATURDAY

SUNDAY

MONDAY

TUESDAY

WEDNESDAY

THURSDAY

FRIDAY

SATURDAY

SUNDAY

Cooper's Hawk

Although broadly distributed, this hawk is not often
seen because it is secretive and inconspicuous,
particularly during the breeding season.

MONDAY

TUESDAY

WEDNESDAY

THURSDAY

FRIDAY

SATURDAY

SUNDAY

Western Tanager

The species is a characteristic bird of North America's western forests and is the continent's most northerly breeding tanager.

MONDAY

TUESDAY

WEDNESDAY

THURSDAY

FRIDAY

SATURDAY

SUNDAY

Painted Bunting

As one of North America's most strikingly
colored songbirds, it more than deserves
its French name, *nonpareil,* which means
"without equal."

MONDAY

TUESDAY

WEDNESDAY

THURSDAY

FRIDAY

SATURDAY

SUNDAY

Barn Owl

One of the most widespread of all
owls, they have versatile nest sites, and an
ability to use human-modified habitats.

Northern Parula

Parula americana

Bird song: *Frrrreep!*

Female

Male

A relatively small, short-tailed, and very active warbler, the Northern Parula breeds through much of the eastern United States and across southeastern Canada. They winter in a variety of different habitats across Mexico and the Caribbean, and travel north to nest in much of the central and eastern United States and Canada. Find them in mixed-species flocks of other warblers.

This delicate-looking bird inhabits forest areas, and although both sexes of this tiny woodland warbler species look alike, Northern Parulas are one of the few that have visible differences between male and female. Both have blue-gray backs with a yellow-green patch in the middle and a yellow band across the breast. However, the females are slightly paler in coloration and have a greener tint to the entire back. Adult males also sport a chestnut breast band.

These birds forage in the middle and top regions of trees at the outermost parts of the foliage, occasionally moving lower to hunt in understory vegetation. Parulas sometimes also take flying insects in the air. Even if you don't see them, you can still hear the ascending, buzzy trill of the males making their presence known.

When they're ready to nest, Northern Parulas prefer mature forests near water. The females use lichen and moss to build a hanging cup. Their nests are so high (sometimes even 100 feet (30 m)) that it's often difficult to study their nesting behavior.

NOTES	SUNDAY	MONDAY	TUESDAY

WEDNESDAY	THURSDAY	FRIDAY	SATURDAY

Northern Parula Facts

Fun fact: They are one of the earliest tropical migrants to the eastern woodlands in the spring. They arrive so early that once you start getting used to them, they'll be ready to head back to their wintering grounds.

Food: At their winter homes, they eat the tender young buds on tree branches, in addition to fruit, nectar, and seeds. During the breeding season, you won't often find them at a feeder because they prefer insects, with spiders and caterpillars as their springtime meal of choice.

Nesting: A mating pair often has one to two broods of two to seven eggs. The eggs range from white to creamy-white and speckled with red, brown, purple, or gray. The nest takes about four days to build, with an incubation period of twelve to fourteen days. The nesting period usually lasts around ten to eleven days.

Bird song: Most Northern Parulas have two types of songs. One, the most frequently produced, is a buzzy, ascending trill; it is thought to have roles in male attraction and communication between mates. The other song type consists of a series of buzzy notes. It is given especially at dawn and dusk and probably plays a role in territorial defense. Both males and females give two brief calls, a *chip* and a *tseep,* which may have aggressive signaling functions, but these calls are used in other contexts as well.

MONDAY

....

TUESDAY

....

WEDNESDAY

....

THURSDAY

....

FRIDAY

....

SATURDAY

....

SUNDAY

....

MONDAY

TUESDAY

WEDNESDAY

THURSDAY

FRIDAY

SATURDAY

SUNDAY

Mississippi Kite

Often, they'll choose a nesting location close to, or
even containing, nests of bees or wasps to help
protect their nestlings from climbing predators.

MONDAY

TUESDAY

WEDNESDAY

THURSDAY

FRIDAY

SATURDAY

SUNDAY

Sandhill Crane

Sandhill Cranes form extremely large flocks—into
the tens of thousands—on their wintering grounds
and during migration.

MONDAY

TUESDAY

WEDNESDAY

THURSDAY

Blue Jay

Although they can be aggressive toward other
birds, they are common in towns and residential
areas, especially with large oaks.

Eastern Bluebird

Sialia sialis

Bird song: *tu-a-wee*

Female

Male

Eastern Bluebirds are much admired and easily recognized thrushes of North America's eastern half. They are known for dwelling in open habitats, often in the vicinity of human settlements, and frequently using nesting boxes.

They breed from Ontario and Manitoba south to Florida through Texas and southeastern Arizona. They prefer open areas with sparse groundcover and scattered trees, such as orchards, parks, and recently cut or burned woods. They eat insects caught on the ground and small fruits taken from bushes and trees.

When the time for nesting arrives in the spring, male Eastern Bluebirds that aren't returning to a previous nest cavity will often hunt for an old woodpecker hole. The males will then attempt to attract females by making their warbling call. Once they have found a female, they will then defend the nesting cavity from any would-be intruders, such as European Starlings, House Sparrows, Tree Swallows, and chickadees.

Frequent vocalizations are their loud and soft songs and the *tu-a-wee*. Loud songs, usually given by males for mate attraction and territorial defense, are rich, low-pitched warbling sounds, something like *tury, cherwee, cheye-ley* or *cyo ala loee—alee ay lalo leeo*. Soft songs, directed by males to their mates, are lower in volume but otherwise similar. *Tu-a-wee* calls, given by both sexes, function to keep family members in contact as they forage.

NOTES	SUNDAY	MONDAY	TUESDAY

WEDNESDAY	THURSDAY	FRIDAY	SATURDAY

Eastern Bluebird Facts

Fun fact: Back in the early twentieth century, populations dropped by nearly 90 percent because of competition for nesting cavities. For a few decades, the males were losing the battle against the most aggressive European Starlings, House Sparrows, Tree Sparrows, and other chickadees. By the 1960s, populations began rising again thanks to the establishment of bluebird trails and more accessible information about nest boxes.

Plumage: While many thrushes in eastern North America are comparatively drab in color, you can't miss an Eastern Bluebird with their striking azure plumage above and wings that contrast beautifully with a rusty red breast.

Close relative: If you're seeking bluebirds out west, try finding a Western Bluebird.

Food: In the fall and winter, bluebirds eat fruit including mistletoe, blueberries, currants, and juniper berries. However, their main prey includes caterpillars, beetles, crickets, grasshoppers, and spiders.

Nesting: These bluebirds choose cavities up to 50 feet (15 m) off the ground. They prefer smaller nests to snuggle up in the fine grasses and sometimes feathers. When it comes to nest boxes, they enjoy snug boxes with a slightly larger entrance hole. Bluebirds may use the same nest for multiple broods, laying eggs of pale blue.

MONDAY

TUESDAY

WEDNESDAY

THURSDAY

FRIDAY

SATURDAY

SUNDAY

MONDAY

TUESDAY

WEDNESDAY

THURSDAY

FRIDAY

SATURDAY

SUNDAY

Mountain Bluebird

Unlike other bluebird species, Mountain
Bluebirds hover while foraging, pouncing on
their insect prey from an elevated perch.

MONDAY

TUESDAY

WEDNESDAY

THURSDAY

FRIDAY

SATURDAY

SUNDAY

Violet-green Swallow

These swallows usually forage in small
groups, flying high over the ground or low
over fields or water.

MONDAY

TUESDAY

WEDNESDAY

THURSDAY

Olive Warbler

A small, fairly common songbird found only
in a highly specialized habitat of mountain pine
forests above 7,000 feet (2.1 km).

Yellow-rumped Warbler

Dendroica coronate

Bird song: *tuwee-tuwee*

Female

Male

Distinguished by its yellow rump, head, and side patches, the Yellow-rumped Warbler is a very common breeding songbird found in Alaska, across most of Canada, and throughout the northeastern United States, as well as parts of the West. Breeding largely in coniferous forests, in its wintering range—over the southern United States and along the West Coast—it occurs in an array of open areas, such as agricultural and residential sites, marshes, and shrublands.

For many of us, Yellow-rumped Warblers will be a winter migrant, visiting feeders, berry bushes, and many other food sources for the winter before heading back northward. They are the only warbler able to digest the waxes found in bayberries and wax myrtles. So keep an eye out for the gray-black males and brownish females when they are in town.

This warbler forages for insects and spiders in trees and often spends portions of its feeding periods catching flying insects while in flight. These birds can cling to vertical bark, similar to woodpeckers and nuthatches, while searching for bugs on tree trunks. During migration and while wintering, they also eat fruit and nectar.

Yellow-rumped Warblers seemingly make do with whatever is available, flitting among the tress for a wide variety of foods. They're happy to dine on many different types of berries and fruits, but they've also been known to swoop down from the trees to feed on the seeds of wild grasses.

NOTES	SUNDAY	MONDAY	TUESDAY

WEDNESDAY	THURSDAY	FRIDAY	SATURDAY

Yellow-rumped Warbler Facts

Food: They enjoy having variety in their diet, flitting among the trees for food. Sometimes they'll cling to the bark in search of insects hiding in the nooks and crannies. They'll also dine on different types of berries and fruit, including bayberries that their other warbler cousins are not able to digest. Sometimes they will even carefully perch among aphids (very small, soft-bodied insects), waiting to drink the sweet honeydew they excrete.

Close relative: A subspecies only found in Mexico and Guatemala is the incredible black-and-yellow Goldman's Warbler.

Nesting: Yellow-rumped Warblers choose between tree species of hemlock, spruce, white cedar, pine, and Douglas fir. They place their nests anywhere from 4 to 50 feet (1.2 to 15 m) high, tucked in close to the trunk. With the male bringing her supplies, the female builds the nest of twigs, pine needles, grasses, and rootlets. Sometimes she will also use moose, horse, and deer hair. Building takes about ten days.

Bird song: Only male Yellow-rumped Warblers sing. Songs vary geographically, but one type consists of a trilling, bell-like sound: *tuwee-tuwee-tuwee* or *tyew-tyew-tyew*. Other songs sound like *sidl sidl sidl seedl seedl seedl*.

Brief calls include a sharp *chek,* uttered when the birds are foraging; *psit,* given in various contexts; a soft *tsee* produced in flight; and metallic *chips* produced when alarmed.

MONDAY

TUESDAY

WEDNESDAY

THURSDAY

FRIDAY

SATURDAY

SUNDAY

MONDAY

TUESDAY

WEDNESDAY

THURSDAY

FRIDAY

SATURDAY

SUNDAY

Orange-crowned Warbler

The most abundant warbler breeding in the
woodlands, they are found most
often along rivers or streams.

MONDAY

TUESDAY

WEDNESDAY

THURSDAY

Scissor-tailed Flycatcher

With a long, elegant tail, the male's is, on average,
3 inches (7.5 cm) longer than his mate's.

MONDAY

TUESDAY

WEDNESDAY

THURSDAY

FRIDAY

SATURDAY

SUNDAY

Eastern Screech-Owl

Found mainly in the eastern half of the United
States, they feed on insects, crayfish, earthworms,
songbirds, and rodents.

MONDAY

TUESDAY

WEDNESDAY

THURSDAY

FRIDAY

SATURDAY

SUNDAY

Caspian Tern

The largest tern, with a strong, graceful flight,
they breed along the Pacific, Atlantic, and Gulf
coasts, as well as along the Great Lakes.

Western Kingbird

Tyrannus verticalis

Bird song: *kip kip kip*

The Western Kingbird is a conspicuous bird of open spaces in the western United States and Canada. It occupies a variety of habitats, including savannas, shrublands, agricultural lands, deserts, woodlands, and even urban areas.

Known as birds of the West, Western Kingbirds tend to wander during the fall migration. Since 1915, they have been regular winter residents in Florida.

The large Western Kingbirds are striking. They choose perches that enable them to easily survey the open areas, such as power lines, barbed wire fences, and lone trees. This flycatcher feeds by capturing flying prey in the air, often with acrobatic maneuvers. Insects make up the bulk of its diet.

Find them in western and central North America during the breeding season. Males find a suitable territory and patrol the borders of it, all while singing a song consisting of a series of sharp *kips* followed by a series of high-pitched notes. Once a female joins him, they search together for a suitable nest tree, then draw back the borders of the territory to a more manageable size and focus on nesting. The female builds the nest on her own while the male keeps watch.

Despite their aggressive behaviors, they are intelligent enough to know the difference between a threat and a fellow neighbor. Western Kingbirds can be found sharing their nest tree with a few other species, including Mourning Doves, grackles, orioles, House Wrens, and others.

NOTES SUNDAY MONDAY TUESDAY

WEDNESDAY	THURSDAY	FRIDAY	SATURDAY

Western Kingbird Facts

Fun fact: Befitting of their reputation for being loud and aggressive, this species can often be seen making loud buzzing calls while chasing away intruders from their territories, such as American Kestrels and Red-tailed Hawks, and even animals that are much larger than they are.

Food: Mainly insectivores, they hunt by sight during the day. They may capture a few insects before returning to their perch, where kingbirds shake or beat them against the perch to subdue them. They also eat terrestrial prey, or sometimes bees and wasps, grasshoppers, butterflies, caterpillars, and spiders.

Nesting: Western Kingbirds build their nests in trees or shrubs such as cottonwood, elm, willow, yucca, big sagebrush, and green ash. The female builds the nest on her own while the male keeps watch. She weaves together grass stems, rootlets, fine twigs, cotton, and other plant fiber into a bulky, open cup. The nest measures about 6 inches (15 cm) across and 4 inches (10 cm) deep, with the inner cup about 2 inches (5 cm) deep.

Bird song: During the breeding season, males produce a song consisting of a series of sharp *kips* followed by a series of high-pitched notes. The probable functions of this song are mate attraction and territorial advertisement. Other vocalizations are *kee-kee*, given by mated pairs; a *pwuh-T*, used by males while patrolling territories and by both sexes while mobbing predators at their nests; and a harsh, buzzing call males use when attacking predators or other kingbirds.

MONDAY

TUESDAY

WEDNESDAY

THURSDAY

FRIDAY

SATURDAY

SUNDAY

MONDAY

TUESDAY

WEDNESDAY

THURSDAY

FRIDAY

SATURDAY

SUNDAY

Carolina Wren

Valuing their chosen spaces, they remain
in the tangled thickets, raising their
offspring in snug little nests.

MONDAY

TUESDAY

WEDNESDAY

THURSDAY

FRIDAY

SATURDAY

SUNDAY

Dickcissel

A sparrow-like bird of the United States' central
prairie region, they prefer open grassland with
dense cover and tallish vegetation.

MONDAY

TUESDAY

WEDNESDAY

THURSDAY

Lazuli Bunting

They forage on the ground, in grasses, shrubs, and
trees, consuming seeds and fruits throughout
the year, and spiders and insects
during the breeding season.

MONDAY

TUESDAY

WEDNESDAY

THURSDAY

NOTES

NOTES

NOTES

NOTES

NOTES

NOTES

NOTES

First published in 2024 by Rock Point, an imprint of The Quarto Group,
142 West 36th Street, 4th Floor, New York, NY 10018, USA
(212) 779-4972 www.Quarto.com

Contains content previously published in 2018 as *Bird Songs* by Epic Ink and in 2024 as *The Mindful Birder's Journal* by Rock Point, imprints of The Quarto Group, 142 West 36th Street, 4th Floor, New York, NY 10018.

Rock Point titles are also available at discount for retail, wholesale, promotional, and bulk purchase. For details, contact the Special Sales Manager by email at specialsales@quarto.com or by mail at The Quarto Group, Attn: Special Sales Manager, 100 Cummings Center Suite 265D, Beverly, MA 01915 USA.

10 9 8 7 6 5 4 3 2 1

ISBN: 978-1-57715-416-7

Group Publisher: Rage Kindelsperger
Editorial Director: Erin Canning
Creative Director: Laura Drew
Managing Editor: Cara Donaldson
Editor: Katelynn Abraham
Cover and Interior Design: Scott Richardson

Printed in China

This book provides general and scientific information on ornithology and their inspirational and holistic benefits. However, it should not be relied upon as recommending or promoting any specific diagnosis or method of treatment for a particular condition, and it is not intended as a substitute for medical advice or for direct diagnosis and treatment of a medical condition by a qualified physician. Readers who have questions about a particular condition, possible treatments for that condition, or possible reactions from the condition or its treatment should consult a physician or other qualified healthcare professional.